Steak & Stations

Michael Egan lives in Liverpool and is a member of Edge Hill University's Poetry and Poetics Research Group. He is the editor of *The Binturong Review*. Michael's poems have appeared in *Erbacce*, *Great Works*, *Zafusy* and *Poetry Salzburg*. A pamphlet, *The River Swam*, was published in 2005 and a second, *Folklores*, in 2010. This is his first full collection.

Steak & Stations
Michael Egan

Penned in the Margins
LONDON

PUBLISHED BY PENNED IN THE MARGINS
53 Arcadia Court, 45 Old Castle Street, London E1 7NY
www.pennedinthemargins.co.uk

All rights reserved

© Michael Egan

The right of Michael Egan to be identified as the author of this work has been asserted by him in accordance with Section 77 of the Copyright, Designs and Patent Act 1988.

This book is in copyright. Subject to statutory exception and to provisions of relevant collective licensing agreements, no reproduction of any part may take place without the written permission of Penned in the Margins.

First published 2010

ISBN
978-0-9565467-5-3

This book is sold subject to the condition that it shall not, by way of trade or otherwise, be lent, re-sold, hired out, or otherwise circulated without the publisher's prior consent in any form of binding or cover other than that in which it is published and without a similar condition including this condition being imposed on the subsequent purchaser.

ACKNOWLEDGEMENTS

Acknowledgements are due to the following publications, in which some of these poems have appeared: *Cake Magazine, Erbacce, Great Works, Pen Pusher.*

Thanks to my wife and family for their support, Robert Sheppard and members of the Poetry and Poetics Research Group, Chris McCabe, my co-editor of *The Binturong Review* Daniel Bevan and my friend and Goodist Alex Holt.

Sam Gunn deserves a mention too for his help with the editing process and suggesting walks to the river.

Contents

Steak

steak!	15
landfall	16
three italians and a spaniard	17
on his collar a blue bell	19
she slapped him	21
all about the floor books were strewn	22
don't the taxis bomb it in wakefield	23
I've had a belli full!	24
the jobless man does nothing...	25
I am no pre-raphaelite	28
gizzards and heart	29
calculations	31
he'd said something at dinner	33
only seen from uncanny angles	34
I lied to the inquisition...	35
monkey of my inkpot	37
at the barber's blade...	39
in lowering cages	41
or back to the page with the gulls	43
fox watcher on island road	44
from here I imagine god's fist might plummet earthwards	45
yellowed tree	47

Crossed Out Stations

free to drink	51
experiential cross	52
some short chronicles	53
on the handkerchief	54
tri-autumn	55
unrobed	56
we put up a calendar with pins	57
d. dumaboc	58

Station Stop

roby	61
edge hill	62
sankey for penketh	63
mossley hill	64
huyton	65
hartford	66
waverley	67

Further Fragments

von zadora-gerlof's skull	71
anglo-australian rice	72
eagles	73
cumberland road	75
after the plough	76
boats	77

For Noelle

Steak & Stations

after all
as the man said
thought
is in de mouf

'A Theory of Poetry', John James

The shadow of a buzzard moving, seldom
Noticed in the city – people
Have lost interest in that sort of thing.

'Some Words about Some Silence', Christopher Middleton

Steak

steak!

they gave him steak   his gums red and hollow
not one tooth left   he chewed it   he swallowed every bit
he got it all ate   can't eat the stuff now
not even soaked in gravy   onions and mushy peas
his mother with her dark eyes from as far east as you can go
not the dingle's sloping streets but nothing foreign about her really
it was just she was weary   that's why her eyes were dark
her hair falling out then   so young   she wore
a grey shawl over her head as if   going to mass
they never did   how strange   them never setting
foot in church   our lot   my mother's lot
always there   day in day out   on first name terms
with the priest   so he blessed my father
before he got new teeth   crossed his hollow
gums   gave him holy water to splash on them
but that steak   massive chunks at the end of his fork
pushed into the blessed memories of how it was to chew.

landfall

it is other than this   these waves we've had
for too long   so long they're ours these unsteady suppers
it has shape   look   the long back of a sleeping
beast   because the river dee has long since silted
we end up here   her legs open   lady waiting
lighthouses flickering in harbours   bays
ports   there is the firm footing of forgotten streets   stumble
cobble   and going further out so you can't see the sea
so you can't smell it   forget what merchants bring
what went back out   why penny lane is penny lane
there's less of it   less of this man's land
of bricks rising up and windows firmly shut   the homely hearths
you know lay at the bottom of those chimneys   chimneys
exhaling smoke   from the hill   to see it is enough
even up there   no sea   just the still waves of land
frozen tumult of fields   and the tall spike
of an aerial   like a mast and all of this its ship
it is other than this   out there   this wind now blowing
and rummaging the grass   wouldn't bother sails
they'd stay and soup wouldn't slosh from our bowls.

three italians and a spaniard

the night before they left   my keys   dug into a beam
carved out *amato* four times   sat finishing the punch
this vision of christmas in wool   fat santa stretched across
his chest   poked my stomach   said *winnie winnie*
that creased him   cried now *mr university will come find me*
he say luigi   luigi you buy new beams   the chair
unsteady   cut my name next to his   earlier the spaniard
had been throwing stones at her window   *lara lara*
he sang her name   me in her bed   her too —
toned legs   ran everyday   could have crushed me
lara lara he went on all night   I remembered his story
on the bank of the seine   a communist thespian   his father
pushed de gaulle or mitterrand   someone   into the river
never allowed into france again   how many
parts did he miss out on for that?   it worked out all right
ended up in an iberian *confessions of a window cleaner*
horny matador   randy conquistador
now   the third italian wore too much make-up
like some roman street whore byron might have knocked
and watching her take that paint off was   to watch
a woman undress   naked she wasn't the same
more like the picture her sister took   in the south
she must have been sixteen   naked   so you saw nothing
she burst in   the spaniard was climbing up   calling calling
had woken her   drunk romeo   juliet's hand on my crotch
bursting in   she was shocked   going after her

santa pulled me into the kitchen   poured me another punch
cried about his sweet shop in the mountains   next morning
the italians left for amsterdam   and I spent two weeks
playing back jack   drinking four euro bordeaux with the spaniard.

on his collar a blue bell

little bell ringing on the landing   morning happens
at the peeling of st.mary's   now it's night
no animal sniffing at the yard to bring on thought
the pigeon has long since flown   first we found it
on the bench   got in a right panic if I went too near
scattered seeds   always a white cat ready to pounce
I banged on the window   the pigeon slept   the cat ran
ours at the window scrabbling   days later that pigeon
managed to hobble to the flower bed   some strangeness
about its beak   the cat kept coming back   and when I tried
to feed the bird   it flapped into the shed   locked in with an urn
then leaving the door ajar   in the morning it was gone
only the church bells and the little bell at the window
sad eyed to find the bird flown   nothing now
like that out there   these alleys are too narrow
great gates at their end so the bins don't get nicked
foxes keep to the park and pester taxi drivers   *you'd
be surprised how many we get*   long ago I could sleep as a child
knowing lions slept too   not so far away   just to hear
a roar in the night a baboon cackle   once we thought we heard
bells   then going outside saw faint lights   heard drums
a distant lightshow   those lights   for michael jackson
singing *bad* almost as exciting as when   with the patio
doors open   next door's dog went suddenly quiet
us eating oranges then we heard it   chris de burgh
definitely him   *lady in red* floating over from the old lord's

estate   that was a moment   when the song ended
the dog was whimpering   his nose poking through
a hole in the fence and at st.michael's on the hill they began
ringing their bells   practised every saturday
listening   we ate so many oranges   peel scattered across crazy
                                                  paving.

she slapped him

she slapped him   froze after her palm met his face
the bedroom was downstairs   everyone
must have heard   it was to stop him going on
the ceiling   hanging newspaper   frogs outside on the pond
someone turned the gas on later at the party   someone kept
leaning on the oven   turning on the gas
so it stank   she was still there
on the bed   he brought her tea   she didn't trust
that they weren't all spitting in the milk   colder and colder
something like that probably happened
strange hands in the fridge   someone stole beans
they found a tin next morning   shoved in
the toilet   a used condom floating on top
god knows what had happened in there
jacob's crackers in the bath   and the shower left on
gas leaking   he pulled the lad away and struggling
they fell against the bedroom door
she woke with the noise   still angry still sorry
the mark not quite gone on his face
him and the lad fell again through the door
forced it open   they fought so much
her half naked   jumped out of bed
the whole party saw her   red eyes   in her
underwear   still gas leaking   it seemed only he noticed
someone else had knocked the hob   as they fell.

all about the floor books were strewn

all about the floor books were strewn
as if no one on earth   cared
enough to shelve them   or they'd grown there
so many   in one there must be something
a week   unopened   the cats started sleeping on them
biting corners   cat eared them   their scratch marks on the covers
you can hear the children outside passing   climbing along the wall
silhouettes against the blinds   back and forth
never their own wall   eggs cracked into the bowl
then realising there was no parmesan   just hardened cheddar
how can you have carbonara without parmesan?
parmesan or garlic? little cloves   wet in the fridge
cut them   they're brown   too green at their core
the little one   the black one with his flat face   drooping whiskers
mews for bacon   paws dirty enough   they tear
covers from beds   hoover and hoover   it's the dust
in the corners that's the worse   takes him four trips
upstairs to get rid of the books   leaves *bel ami* where it fell
read it once in a mock tudor pub   whiskeys   all doubles
and not lager   because of the taste on his breath   sure to kiss   until
she called him   a different she   was ready when he got to her
she let the robe fall   they had little time.

don't the taxis bomb it in wakefield

don't the taxis bomb it in wakefield   said the drummer
tapping   ponytail loose so he hardly looked himself
his eyes sharper   behind glasses   each hill
a nightmare   then down   on the train
rickety   facing each other though they'd only
just that minute been introduced   *beth* and the other
both irish   not a hint of accent   how running for the train
rain began   beneath a railway bridge was a small off licence
even this   strange   without question a bag full
of lager and fags   too much haze
amidst that haze came drowsiness   leant his head
against her leg   snored   tasted her tights   purple
so they shot down the hill too fast to take in the town
wakefield might have been hull   rotherham
or bolton   like when noodles spilled from the take away
the police horse trampling through it
hemmed in like a riot   slowly the train crawling away
and wandering then   it all looked the same
any place at night seems that   walking   just shut-up shops
and the cold taxi ranks   emptying bars   some hard case
getting battered   but in the morning in wakefield
his head was in an ashtray   walking to the station
they could see the town   taxis bombed past them
their legs ached   it seemed such a steep place
playing poker on the train back   the drummer pointed
to the new football stadium   said *mcalpine* against his reflection.

I've had a belli full!

I've had a belly full of it   all of it
a half grinning gargoyle   I know
no streets such as his   peering down on poverty
rutting a cousin against a confessional   when I've
walked through town smoking   shattered telephone box
nothing so lurid   portly angels kept eating
she   some girl I'd found   pissed without care
on the phone   stream of words   outside a thud
falling   some lad had jumped from the second floor   landed
in a thorn bush and lay there crying   when we left the room
there was only the blanket they'd hung on the wall
earlier a too beautiful girl   they   cheering us on like a football
match   earlier still   my own fall   leaping a broken fence
I hardly noticed   not even the blood on the black seat
of the taxi   tore my trousers   arse on show
cheering   her hand lingering there   *you've got an
amazing arse*   might as well have looked down at me from a carriage
condemned me to death   when I asked father I said
father I should probably confess some stuff   that came up
that and the sun on renshaw street   deserted apart from
a tramp sitting in his own piss calling *solomon solomon*
when I ignored him he called again   *solomon solomon*
and there above me a grinning statue   leering from *lewis's*
his tiny ding-a-ling pecker nob dirty-dangler
on display   no doubt in his head some thought
of nook-and-crannys chuffs   love canals dirty ditches.

the jobless man does nothing   watches sky sports news all day

took his arms gave them to one whose hands were tired from toil
he'd done nothing with them for months made tea
flicked channels   *while we're at it*   *why keep his eyes?*
signed the form scooped them out gave them to a sad soul
a refugee who'd seen too much a straight swap
he sat watching sky sports news always always
in the corners of his eyes bodies cadavers of another's memory
and when they gave his ears to a banker who'd lost his own
in a mafia hit he could hear faintly first *where's the money*
where's the money over *birmingham have signed* *burnley*
have signed unveiling new players he couldn't look bodies
were piling up around him his vision a red mist with no hands
to cover his eyes next they gave his eyelids to a baby born
without any *you don't need them* they told him *you've done*
nothing for months *sit there* *sign here* stared on and on
couldn't change the channel they offered his legs to a soldier
back from basra his dad told him it was the right thing to do
couldn't complain since they'd took out his tongue for a politician
who'd bit hers off talking her way out of why she'd spent
four thousand a month on window tax though she lived in a chic
apartment one west facing window *the way things are*
said his dad *let's face it you've not a chance of finding*
a job *we need a few bob that's all* *just sit there* *we'll bring you tea*
poor soldier had to work hard to build up such lazy muscles
ran a marathon at christmas he saw it on sky sports news

couldn't help but look   couldn't hear what was said
where's the money   where's the money   all of london
red   woozy   he saw the uniform   the familiar ankles   the scar
just below the left knee   would have cried   it was autumn
when they'd given his tear ducts to a mother who'd cried too much
for her   lost daughter   *she'll never see her again*
you can't deny her grief   signed with a pen in his mouth
felt strange against his gums   teeth knocked gently out
last tuesday because there are so many who need them
the gap toothed   the woman who longs to crunch crackling
the man who dreams of biting blackpool rock
all you do is sip tea through a straw   and finally he woke
one morning   though he hardly slept these days
where's the money   where's the money screamed
throughout the night   the day   he woke   propped up on the couch
barnsley have signed   blackburn have signed   the newsreaders
tinged with red   shadows of bodies just out of sight
begging him   listened listened   for what had always been
there   knew they'd never take   the ever slowing beat
it'd hardly seemed worth beating these months   but did
listened   nothing   just *brentford have signed*   and looking
down saw where they'd opened him up   a little battery
there   draining away   they came later   sat on the armchairs
eating their chips from newspaper   *you didn't need it*
you've been sat there months   just wasting it
and anyway this recession'll never lift   don't you
watch the news?   no need for men like you anymore
just sit there   rest   that battery'll last till sunday
at least   don't worry we'll change it saturday

sat there   waited   then saturday afternoon
the new season kicked off   his tea cold
empty mugs everywhere   they came in with their chips
somehow the battery had fallen out   leaked over the carpet
and his eyes were moist   someone guessed it had to be tea
wouldn't taste it   put him in a tesco bag   turned off the tv.

I am no pre-raphaelite

I am no pre-raphaelite   have no certain ideas to express
saw a fox crushed by a wheel   felt nothing more than
sorrow for that fox   did not linger there to look
the same as the dog   limping   yanked on a chain
with a deep scar across his muzzle   from fighting
they do that round here   on waste ground   under
the bridge   so many their whimpers cross the river
only drowned out by the sirens in the freight
yard   the yellow lifter taking hold   a blue box
pulled out of the mass   in a penny arcade
desperate for the small toy   it was a bear   studied it
then let the grapple loose   never got hold of it
and spent the rest of the afternoon trying to tip the coins
one drops   pushes the others   my brother
sure it's magnetised   they cling to each other
will not drop   heave back   heave back lads
and when last winter there were heavy winds   a crane
toppled   crushed a freight   the last one to be lifted
and startled the gulls who had settled on its roof
the crane breaking in two   fell into the river
began to float   millais' *ophelia*   except her face
sharp   sank somewhere near hale   where the land stinks.

gizzards and heart

he made a mousse of pig heart and a confit of duck
gizzards   her dress   little blackbirds   white on black
she wore a garter   and her neck so perfumed
he set the starter down   glistening trotters
a cider and toenail sauce   she swooned
her hand touched his   she wore the ring
he bought her   the day they had the finest
snout they'd ever tasted   an earlobe cream
on the side   he tried to copy that   with wasabi spiced
little crisp bits of ear   it'd taken him an afternoon
to burn away the hairs   that's how she knew he
loved her   and the blood pudding sorbet came next
a palate cleanser   she was blushing   wanted to take him
to bed as he spooned the mousse   all the arteries
discarded   just the best bits of the heart   the parts
that loved   loved to wallow in mud as she loved
to lay in his arms   they both knew as he lifted
the gizzards   knew they'd not sleep   but lick
each other's necks   bite each other's chests   breast
of seagull on the side   a masala beak tower
they couldn't speak   eyes never left each other
as they ate   he poured the sweet wine for dessert
told her it was a parasite that caused the sweetness
she joked   he was her parasite   she was sweet for him
and the dessert was sweeter   quenelles of caramelised
nightingale   he sang to her as he served   dusted

chocolate ants across the top   for crunch   she devoured
it   her hands could hardly stop   she dug her nails into his palms
he barely winced   begged her to dig harder
they moaned as they poured cream over the little birds
she tasted cinnamon and cardamom   it was moroccan
he told her   she let her toes dance up his leg
and there wasn't time for *casu marzo*   that delicious illicit cheese
he'd flown in specially   they were intoxicated with each other
needed no dead maggots to drug them   she leapt
across the table   mousse and sorbet all over her
pretty dress   he tore that off and made love there
her fingers keeping hold of a gizzard   her garter torn   as he
told her he loved her   said   you are my beast   you are my monster.

calculations

and the gas pipe reeks it stretches
across the railway track   up there
a boy died   found fallen to the platform
up here a man   bomber jacket
grey hair   like he'd had too much of civil
service   like his suit was hung up at home
a wife waiting with mash potatoes crusting
over and the gravy drying   bacon tap it
it'd shatter   little shards they'd call
it pancetta dust at that restaurant we went to
on the docks   one of those mild winter
evenings I ordered steak   expected fries
at least   not even mustard on offer
when it came I'd never tasted a steak so well
salted   rock salt sprinkled over   perfect
but not a chip in sight   *carlos will sort it out*
said the waiter   he had a spiv's moustache
like my uncle in the picture   1942 munitions
factory in london   all his girls around him
and somewhere in that mass was the girl
he left his wife for   probably seduced her
in danish dutch flemish he could speak
all the useless languages   this man
wisps of whitening hair   smoke yellowed fingers
sat with his back against the wall   the gas pipe
behind the wall   the railway winding off

sudden siren from the river   a calculator
in his hand   tapping away   sat in a pool
of water   though it hadn't rained   I stopped
there was a bike in the road and I noticed his
head was cut   he tapped wildly away   numbers
debts   a smashed vodka bottle   *are you ok?*
but a train passed then   he lifted his head
then looked to the numbers   keys   the train
wouldn't stop at the next station   still closed
since the boy fell   I asked again and this time he heard.

he'd said something at dinner

the next night   dinner was at an italian bistro
north john street   we went down into it
and drank more than ate   did both slowly
it was still light when we came out   lighting up
offering him one   a crowd of tourists
all tanned   olive skinned   peered up
at the beatles statues   grotesque   silence
carried over from last night   my fault of course
I'd drank too much   the limoncello that was a gift
and then got them all to take a scotch   what I'd said
still sticking in their throats   still something else
needed to be said   I drank the idea away
same as we all did in the restaurant   but coming out
the four of us waiting for a taxi   I said
I don't think I'm wrong   you know
he lit up   scowled   a tramp with cupped hands
waiting for coins   looked at me   *what*
he began then left it   kicked a beer can
the tramp had probably been saving   a dirty
hand reached out   slurred something   it had
to be said   confirmed   I told her later
you couldn't expect me to leave it   she would
switch off the light and turn away   proof
positive   the bolognese repeated on me
as I closed my eyes   some guilt that I'd ordered veal.

only seen from uncanny angles

towers of bologna   odd turret   out of place
hidden   of these bus top views
where I seldom sit   too low the ceiling
like   gardens of stone   a show of revolving doors
the guts of offices   and where pigeons perch
crumbling tenements   now brasseries
boutiques   their insides opened
on the civic surgeon's table   spiralled
cast iron stairs   the cracked glass
both stained and plain   cleared tower blocks further out
waiting for hovels to fall   and here
an unused garden   around it   the same
only seen from uncanny angles.

I lied to the inquisition   told them my tea cup was the grail

a french priest so bloated   breath rancid
and stripped me   manacles held me
what they wrote must have made torquemada
weep   it was pg tips   I'd said
two sugars and I'd dunked a digestive in
even a jaffa cake   christ I might have
sucked up the tea of the lord through a kit kat
they burnt me then   held the poker close
told me I was sick   I said *I'm sicker*
than you think   I'd invited muslims
jews   a middle aged baha'i woman
to my tea party   I'd even let a queer
pour   that got them going   they crushed
my fingers so I'd never hold a tea cup
again   then   *where's the cup* they screamed
but I made it last   kept it up till they got me on the rack
for boasting I'd let a whore use the cup
as a piss pot   his face a big blister about to pop
wet   sweaty hair   his teeth hardly any left
the ones that remained bit his lip   stomped
about the dungeon   he called for water then
let it drip on my face for two days   always
close to drowning   I said *it's just like when*
my friend the cathar poured cold tea from my teacup
over me   when all I wore was a crucifix

oh he loved that cup   for that they trussed
me up and put me in a jumpsuit   paraded me
in front of all the other heretics   the one who said
the grail was his hip flask   filled it with gin   the hiker
who claimed the grail was in his rucksack   swaddled
in dirty socks   his sandwiches going mouldy
and the white bearded ancient templar who
cried daily   begged god to release him   held
a cracked and dull chalice   a strange pulsing
light shining from it   but I was the real show
they screamed *where's the cup* as they poked
me with cattle prods   eventually on the fortieth
day I couldn't take it   I was laughing so much
said *ok ok I'll tell you   get your quills ready
lads   dip deep*   they salivated   the french one
got on his knees   held a bible out   spat the our father
dribbled hallelujah   shook and from the smell
I'm sure he pissed himself   I waited
timings always been my thing   waited
and then just as thunder rolled   just as god came down
to hear my joke   I said *I've given it away   left it
with a bag of blouses   corduroy trousers and tartan tank tops
in an oxfam halfway up bold street   in liverpool.*

monkey of my inkpot

he has a sulphurous fart   so I give him
beef supplements each day   a big syringe
in his mouth   he wriggles   but it's not
food he needs   he's not bothered
about the terrible pains in his stomach
it's a nice drink he's after   black ink
to quench his thirst   keeps staring at my
pen   little dots of ink on the page
but nothing more   and he lies by the door
so I can't get out   eyes   big and red and tired
every now and again a trumpet call to keep
me awake   the smell does the trick
but nothing gets written   I pull books
from the shelves just to steal an idea
start on a god who sweats when it's cold
a rain bird drinking up lakes   lame men
ignorant of what they perpetuate   start
on that   the man wakes   says *I'm a pillar
of the universe*   then dies   the monkey
shakes his head   all that I've written is a dot
the page is scattered with them   he whimpers
I turn to newspapers   there's jfk in martha's
vineyard   and a child jumping on a trampoline
an afghan with a purple finger   toothlessly smiling
and dancing south africans clutching vuvuzelas
I can hear the baby next door crying   but there're no

words in her tears   just dot dot dot on the page
when I offer him a suckle on a biro
he shakes his head   too well mannered
he's waiting   *our great to the n-th grandmother*
I finally write   pawing at new scientist
was a hungry sponge larva   she'd sit
knitting amoebas   wrapped in a shawl
of primordial gunk   fairy and rock cakes
going stale in the larder   it's a poor effort
but it's written   he farts with excitement
and clambers over me   sulphur wafting
his arse right by my nose   as I hold the pen
to his mouth   *drink it all*   I tell him
I'll write nothing else all day   not now
when I need to buy mince and tomatoes for dinner
he doesn't listen   his fur dripping with ink
little dots falling to the page   obscuring the poem.

at the barber's blade   his window smashed

he wears a hair band   smokes where
the roads divides   where buses hurtle
and divide again no doubt
further along   towards the mock standing
stones   lit purple   in evening
to welcome drivers off the bridge
fractals   stuttering branches   like
the opening of scissors   blade to blade
holds it there for a moment   smelling
of tobacco   all my barbers have smelt
of tobacco   a woman sweeping around
my face exposed   seeming larger   in my mind
I have less of a face   not so round   now face
against face   I see it expand   just the weight
off   he promises   the weight off and the curls cut
begins   blades meeting and parting   the floor
carpeted   they were once deepest black   whitby jet
now grey and auburn   fracturing towards white
it falls away   and on a shelf   in the mirror
there are rows of tubs   pomades   creams
waxes   and fibre   he shows me my two
sides   *see how your one face fractures*
into two parts   I've taken the curls
his pocket's full of all the curls he's ever taken
his own hair wild   something persian
about him   a xerxes with clippers   and standing I lie

that's just what I wanted   outside
a bus hurtles   workmen are fracturing tarmac
with a hydraulic hammer   their conversation
over it   stuttered   broken and both men frown
they point   to the smashed window
little rivers and streams   a great lake in one corner.

in lowering cages

cake!   all kinds of cake   like madeira
softer and sweeter at its edges   battenburg's
marzipan intrusion   bakewells hiding beneath
that same blanket and let them eat it with tea
better when it's tepid   bits of dundee
soaking up   she can't stop bringing
them in   hear her rummaging cupboards
mixing up a scone   *we've got no currants*
she's keeping her masses happy   like
17th century paris   all toothless   and scratching
flea ridden scalps   doth their wigs and lift
their skirts   not even out of sight
a girl gets ridden four times while they round
the cats up   take a kitten from its mother's
teat   they put them in cages and lighting a fire
they lower each cage   one by one
the cats scratch at the bars   turn and turn
we were greedy for cake   and the stench
all around   must have faded   gotten used
to   like their own stench   all huddled together
kid themselves it's for the fire's warmth
but oh wait till you see the little buggers burn
they don't half yowl   wouldn't you love to
do that to them cats that keep you up all night
and here they go   lowering   burning
little paws dancing   and the sound! it's a song

for the masses to dance to   their laughter
dances   like   the laughter of everyone on
that bus when we slowed by the pubs
and a drunk man   dirty   tramp's beard
stains on his tracksuit bottoms   staggered
towards the bus   and just like that the driver
shut the doors   the drunk swayed
then fell back   grabbed at air his clawed hands could never grasp
and didn't we all laugh   us who were coming
back from nights out   I'd smelt nothing
but booze all the way from crosby   this   the same
as when   in lowering cages   they pleased the masses.

or back to the page with the gulls

herring gulls   I thought   but it was summer
I'd been told they fly towards mountains
away from fishermen   for peace over peaks
black headed gulls on decks   on masts
on unused warehouses   eyeing
dropped chips   and rain clouds rolling over
or there is wales   blackened out
by full-bellied clouds the same sharp movement
of hands grabbing ice creams   queues jostling
into post offices   bodies in bed
in the night   when the storm finally came
greed the same   and greedily wanted by both
when her husband was away   and their eyes dart
over the river   then out to a dark   slumbering
outline of hills   half hidden behind curtains
or back to the page   to the underlined *larus argentatus*
smeared with coffee   its submissive courtship unreadable.

fox watcher on island road

of rumours of foxes   signs of their coming
in wet morning mud   the pawed at   scavenged for
evening   he pulls out dinner scraps from the kitchen bin
fills a tesco bag   meat   bare bones and browning mince
red football cap   his father's toolbox torch
taped there   to peer   in the night at the foxes he knows are waiting
meat scattered   around the park's boundary
beside bollards and hedges   joggers and late-shift
workers don't see him flinging   hiding in bushes
searching for russet flashes   gulls peck at his fox-bait
mingled amongst the rotting meat of weeks past
here   in the shadows between branches
beetles and moths   unwitnessed   strange striped arachnids
bide their hunger   but his foxes never come
just rumours that is all   they tell him
there are many stray dogs around the park   hungry for meat
his torch shows   thousands of eyes   staring back
I'm here till morning he tells me   lighting his cigarette
passes my matches back   *those eyes   there are so many
watching me all night*   offers me some meat from his bag.

from here I imagine god's fist might plummet earthwards

there is the bitten at minaret   wallace's monument
though he was welsh if you peeled away enough
layers of kilt   it was early evening   that time
when the land is opened up   by the contrast
of fading light   and of dispersing clouds   shadowing
hills   and up we drove my throat clogging even then
wound our way to the top where men stood all day
directing cars   they saw it all   the world
at dawn from east to west   a panoramic nightmare
no wonder stirling castle was so hard to take
half an army might fall to its knees up there
just by seeing the laid out land   all of it
and too much of it   I couldn't stand it
retreated to a tea house   for a scone
and coffee   she put her usually so calming
hand   her wonderfully pale   soft   on mine
it did nothing   I could feel the world at my back
the dipping sun   its red cast about the tea room
framed by the window   I took bite after bite
of scone   clogging   I thought the cream will
do the trick but it clogged too and the tea was
still too hot to wash it away   later   walking back
to the coach I had to stop   lean against
a wall   clutch my head   like a mad man
a fool   she said I looked like prince

then started singing *purple rain*   and
thankfully the clouds came again   covered   but even
sitting on the coach   driving down from
that lonely castle I couldn't stop looking out
thinking that this was such a vulnerable place   how
from here I imagine god's fist might plummet earthward.

yellowed tree

where did that yellowed tree come from?
unnoticed beside the conservatory
where others are brittle   and losing leaf
like hokusai's waves
determined fingers grasping
like that planet   with its long day
where all the trees grow towards its sun
the tree sprawls   like cinder toffee
bubbling from an unwatched pan
and reading at my desk   the yellow
merges with the dusk   and the wind
that lifts and disturbs those leaves
a breeze that comes with slight rain
is like the waves falling on the shore
rushing up through shingle
against the pier wall and the whale bone
washed white   then flung back into the sea.

Crossed Out Stations

free to drink

flogged twice   this repeated offence
to not confess   to piss on war memorials
quote the drunk
quote the action of drinking
quote the process of swallowing   gulp
quote that acquittal   release
the breath comes out into a cylinder
falling to the floor   dropping all the carried burdens
have another   a second bitter
you're not *armenian*
swallow   consume   be of that consumption
and consume for others   then fall later.

experiential cross

glass against glass   box within box
simple wall cross to keep and hold
defines   just right for hanging
up   off   from
in its own   with its whiteness
in its own   with its wrapping
take from   take with   take this
and drill it in to place
aside   one is wood   one wooden
another steel   stolen   one with D-A-V-I-D
written across   and all things
get remembered   forgotten
end up in another box
beneath   away   hidden in a cave.

some short chronicles

noting the overlap and lack
telltale signs
the mariner guided by stars
storms at his knees
gales and waves   when he fell
and drowned
here are his chronicles
they fall   are sure to fall again
sure to drop down
cast down   black at the back
take a stake in the probability
it was always going to be
be again.

on the handkerchief

gold leaf   peeled away
what a cheap trick
and pious
our hands
another station to stop at   wait there
this one
humanity
unveiled   salvation left
when contrasted with bright
stainless   light
stained hands
what else have they touched?
uncovered bodies   peeled away
last night   her body
pushing against his   against
the mattress   to avoid touching
closed legs   kisses that pull away
the cloth dropped and trampled.

tri-autumn

each letter is a request
all of it   give   before the bell
fell on monday
downgraded   to noodles and sin
amongst ramen   between the king prawn
and tofu   each leaf of green tea
falling to bed
they fucked
your long journey
look at the crowd gathering in the square
the christmas wheel
and that one man   hair line higher
yellow back pack
stumbling through the fountains.

unrobed

basilica   glass leaded
in segments
said kurds stripped her
the chocolate
wrapper   the half open bin bag
the unfolded scarf
the fallen door
when I unbuttoned the shirt
there was the vest   tight
a chest for smoking
and cut that away   out
a mark on my stomach
at least the heat lessens
the bedclothes fall   we saw a minaret
in the distance   and in a field
below   a man running
as if his life depended on it
harsh sun at his back.

we put up a calendar with pins

fixed to it   the nail gun
pushing each nail into the upturned couch
webbing   fix or do   he comes to the door
recognises the wood   black like tar
like a newly rolled road
shattered with an iron club
and how men stumble
from garston old road down by the park
dragging the frame of a bed
boggy field   his legs cut up
then left it where they'd lit a bonfire
these nails as mementos   bent and useless
left to hang.

d. dumaboc

if you saw graves decked in fragrance
some childhood memory
of incense   you were looking
at some chinese ancestor
in your eyes   filtered through
bread   cheese   crudités and hummus
the goal of all chick peas   this smooth
paprika dusted   evolve
from time   to time
light incense instead of candles
two for the dead   with a design
of a crude symbol   for fruits
those scents between the gravestones
come forward and back   are appeased
for the names below and covered
in fragrance   I know some who do it
but I don't   preferring sleep.

Station Stop

roby

a half memory of its derivation   border farm   boundary settlement

like the nearby river   its rip current deceptive   once a boundary
ragged northumberland to the north   neglected mercia south
another name for that long water then   forgotten

when the train leaves huyton
and not stopping passes by that station with its one lonely man
waiting there since 1932   the awnings   the bluebells

rabi   a manor held by uctred   split for isabel de lathom's love.

edge hill

abandoned   the tunnels with cages and stopping   waiting

my own reflection   avoided
the complications of found engineering equations
of thermodynamics left with the *metro*

I left the nth degree in 1996
left it with the too pungent smell of deep fried fish
thick sickly batter   fingers stained   forever smelling of vinegar

jolting   this is us leaving   reversed arrival   all faces distorted.

sankey for penketh

out of the snow the towers rose still puffing smoke

returning from sankey   a girl asked for a ticket to maghull
and got off far too early   climbed into the wind at hunts cross
a bloated mum told her high skirted daughter to *make men want her*

beneath the ice there is a stifled spring
waiting for late afternoon when the snow should stop
it falls on into the night   covers roads   blankets buds

the towers are markers in the distance   billowing into white.

mossley hill

down an iced-up pathway   ticket office closed but still they queue

step firmly forward   stretch your leg
make the gap small   sit across from the indian girl
with her tight pencil skirts   read kundera   read *time* magazine

the front page littered with great faces   all boxed off and separated
creased   the ice of a threatening jolt to   the climate cracks
on another page an expanding sun   solar storms licking out

a man slips   the heavy sound of   his fall against ice.

huyton

how the curved road beckons   blinds   binds

out back the fallen fences   limp   arboreal windows
showing thorny weeds winding through other gardens
hacked at   a mesh of angles   throw a net over that writhing beast

pull it onto the boat   further upstream is a place to rest and stay
high on clay waves   preserved   it is pulled from the earth this relic
beneath the railway bridge   no longer going viking

keening of the liverpool train through arches   that last
                                                 groan of time.

hartford

in the hanging gate   purring   soft palate that never gets milk

and the lovers are fucking in their lunch break
her on top   him all fingers   eyes on a reduced range rover
her saying later *I couldn't get at it*   breathless in the passenger seat

it stays like the crunch of scattered grit after sleet
each shuffled foot echoing a might-have-been slip
this was all it was   a slip of words   not a declaration of an end

pads to another car bonnet   contented half closed eyes
                                        sip of chartreuse.

waverley

our rich chocolate fudge   left to melt for seven years in constant
                                summer

a dram each and one for the goth with his line of shots
each one followed up with a necked pint   his undulating gullet
and the barmaid's thighs like athenian pillars   this hard doric lust

I wanted to say   *you are all the sweetness I need*
but instead said *let's go for mussels   lots of mussels in big metal buckets*
get drunk on cheap wine   check out far too late and imagine

the old town winking down and all the flowers in the botanic gardens
                                blooming.

Further Fragments

von zadora-gerlof's skull

as good a place as any
to find finely crafted teeth
plates   the cleft suggesting maleness

and yet mine is not so precious
against closely cut grass
without fragrance   scorched

it opens like a jaw
instead of words   light
and heat express themselves

in the first instance of waking
I sit and see   cheese laden
a *harrison dairies* van pass

behind this comes a tractor
slow   without harvest
aware of the road's curve

the driver   mopping his brow
a day for sweat given reign   because
what little clouds there were have passed.

anglo-australian rice

arthritic hands and knees   their grasps and creaks
here is a blurring of borders   of where they cut coal

of where they worked the river   rung it
of its liver hue   and horses have left the yard now

only a plaster horseshoe obscured by scaffolding remains
old doors broken up   so shattered ends

come at angles out of skips   dialect and stress
mimicry   tripping over syllables

ink flows like that worked river   the red that was left
has blackened and mixed with tide washed clay

down comes a barge loaded with images
up comes a ferry full of language.

eagles

even now she is a serial seductress
courtesan of the council estates

I'll have your lips   kiss her russian neighbours
so vast and unknown   no *gulags* to threaten

spit out dialect   one head meets one pavement
curbed   conversation stops

repetition without reaction
aren't there drier places and newer movements?

chisels hit fragile walls
I have music   fall the chisel   halt   fall

dry stone and garrisons
a train can be taken through wild plains

to a gate   where they left guards from colder lands
to shiver and follow eagles north

this island wasn't a shock
it was a chill wind   carving borders

what was missed?
witnesses spoke for the commissioned and destroyed

falling she dances to reveal her body
does it matter if one eye sees her?

if another copies that sensation ?
light alone creates an image

at her touch all voices shout to have a say
caressed   she murmurs   until her lips crack.

cumberland road

as we came on air   the arabic news
was broadcast   midnight

growth and spurt   the sea reclaimed
islands fashioned into life   new tides

and hands given work   washing away old mentors
from this point there is only regeneration

a net cast over homes   silken   brittle
and at this angle they pass over abandoned terraces

framed by leaves and thoughts of collusion
waiting for rain to darken the horizon.

after the plough

when the plague came   allegory
into the dark forest   a vast and deep sky
descending   a faint reflection

he spoke   in the discount furniture store
what a speech!   a damn homily!
market workers gazed   and gawped

within glass and eye   came recognition
in a separate instance   a city was dreamt
it scurried from the riverbank to the bridge

unbroken progress   replicated through song
once similar   it did not matter where we sat
stone or the unploughed field

our bodies longed for rest   the hay was baled
we had food   we had wine and our animals slept
beneath a gilded sky   and the lost pastoral.

boats

late evening   the harbour is speckled with boats
running to the water's edge   as the tide grew
we saw them   unending ships with gaping beast heads

an image too strong is the rod bound with the blade
now grown they have awareness of its purpose
still they toy with the bundle like children

in the lack is his diagram   loose and random
sprawling towards realism   never given
could not last   my beautiful cell   full of energy

and we have not had such a clear night
since the post office   closed
only a fever   delirium   not a definite end.

www.ingramcontent.com/pod-product-compliance
Ingram Content Group UK Ltd.
Pitfield, Milton Keynes, MK11 3LW, UK
UKHW042004230426
12048UKWH00009B/537